BETWEEN THE LEAVES

Anatoly Kudryavitsky
editor

BETWEEN THE LEAVES
An Anthology of New Haiku Writing from Ireland

ARLEN HOUSE

Between the Leaves

is published in 2016 by
ARLEN HOUSE
42 Grange Abbey Road
Baldoyle, Dublin 13
Phone: 353 86 8207617
Email: arlenhouse@gmail.com
arlenhouse.blogspot.com

Distributed internationally by
SYRACUSE UNIVERSITY PRESS
621 Skytop Road, Suite 110
Syracuse, NY 13244–5290
Phone: 315–443–5534/Fax: 315–443–5545
Email: supress@syr.edu

978–1–85132–159–9, paperback

Introduction and selection © Anatoly Kudryavitsky, 2016
Original haiku © individual authors

The moral right of the authors has been asserted

Typesetting by Arlen House

Cover image: *Autumn Leaves* by Anatoly Kudryavitsky
Copyright © Anatoly Kudryavitsky, 2016

Arlen House acknowledges support from

Irish Haiku Society

Contents

7   *Acknowledgements*

9   Introduction
       Anatoly Kudryavitsky

17   Michael Andrew
19   Amanda Bell
21   Pat Boran
22   Paul Bregazzi
23   Jim Burke
24   Marian Burke
25   Patrick Gerard Burke
26   David Burleigh
27   Paul Casey
28   Marion Clarke
30   Marie Coveney
31   Kara Craig
33   Tony Curtis
35   Patrick Deeley
36   Ann Egan
37   Gilles Fabre
39   Helen Farrell Simcox
40   Anton Floyd
42   William Gibb Forsyth
43   Michael Gallagher
44   Patricia Groves
45   Francis Harvey
46   Noragh Jones
48   David J. Kelly
50   Noel King
52   Anatoly Kudryavitsky
54   Leo Lavery
56   Mark Lonergan
57   Aine Mac Aodha

58	Séan Mac Mathúna
60	Clare McCotter
62	Joe McFadden
63	Beth McFarland
65	Séan McWilliams
67	Giovanni Malito
69	Maire Morrisey-Cummins
71	Barbara Morton
72	James Norton
74	Seán O'Connor
76	Terry O'Connor
78	Vincent O'Connor
80	Hugh O'Donnell
82	Siofra O'Donovan
83	Nora O'Dwyer
84	Mary O'Keeffe
85	Eamonn T. O'Neill
86	Teresa O'Neill
87	Kate O'Shea
88	Séamus Barra Ó Súilleabháin
92	Maeve O'Sullivan
94	Thomas Powell
96	Isabelle Prondzynski
98	Mark Roper
99	Gabriel Rosenstock
103	Adam Rudden
104	Michael Scott
106	John W. Sexton
108	Eileen Sheehan
110	Breid Sibley
111	Bee Smith
112	Martin Vaughan
114	Aisling White
116	Mary White
117	About the Authors

Acknowledgements

Acknowledgements are due to the publishers of the following, where some of these poems first appeared: *3lights, A Hundred Gourds, A New Ulster* (Lapwing Press), *Acorn, Asahi Shimbun, Blithe Spirit, Burning Bush 2, Cattails, Chrysanthemum, Creatrix, Daily Haiga, Frogpond, Frozen Butterfly, The Galway Review, The Haiga Pages, Haiku News, Haiku Reality, Haiku Scotland, Haiku Spirit, Haiku World, Heron's Nest, Kernels, Mainichi Daily News, Modern Haiku, Nightingale, Notes from the Gean, Paper Wasp, The Pickled Body, Poetry Haiku, Presence, Prune Juice, The Puffin Review, Red Dragonfly, Roadrunner, Shamrock, Snapshots, Speed Bump Journal, tinywords, Under the Basho, Woodpecker, World Haiku Review, Antlered Stag of Dawn* by Gabriel Rosenstock (The Onslaught Press, 2015), *Aran Currach* by Tony Curtis (Real Ireland Design, 2013), *Because of the Seagull* by Gilles Fabre (Fishing Cat Press, 2005), *Collected Poems* by Francis Harvey (Dedalus Press, 2007), *The Fragrance of Dust* by James Norton (Alba Publishing, 2012), *Let Silence Speak* by Seán O'Connor (Alba Publishing, 2016), *Our Shared Japan* (Dedalus Press, 2007), *Pilgrim Foxes* by James Norton, Sean O'Connor and Ken Jones (Pilgrim Press, 2001), *Pony* by Tony Curtis (Occasional Press, 2013), *The New Haiku* (Snapshot Press, 2002), *Shapshot Press Haiku Calendar 2016, Samoborski Haiku Susreti* (Matrix Croatica Samobor, 2015), *Stone Circles* by Noragh Jones (Pilgrim Press, 2004), *A Train Hurtles West* by Maeve O'Sullivan (Alba Publishing, 2015), *Undercurrents* by Amanda Bell (Alba Publishing, 2016), *Waveforms* by Pat Boran (Orange Crate Books, 2015), *A Year about the Farm* by Michael Scott (Hub Editions, 2013). Poems by Francis Harvey are reprinted by kind permission of the Harvey family and Dedalus Press.

New Haiku from Ireland

Anatoly Kudryavitsky

Originally nature-oriented Japanese short-form poetry which thrived in the seventeenth century, haiku experienced colossal growth in popularity in the English language towards the end of the last century. According to Professor Haruo Shirane:

> while haiku in English is inspired by Japanese haiku, it cannot and should not try to duplicate the rules of Japanese haiku because of significant differences in language, culture and history ... Haiku in English is a short poem, usually written in one to three lines, that seeks out new and revealing perspectives on the human and physical condition, focusing on the immediate physical world around us, particularly that of nature, and on the workings of the human imagination, memory, literature and history.[1]

The history of haiku on the island of Ireland goes back only a few decades, so the development of the genre started relatively late. A few early haiku by Juanita Casey and one by Patrick Kavanagh, all written in the 1960s, were included in *Bamboo Dreams* (Doghouse Books, 2012), the first anthology that documented the history of Irish haiku, and so were miniatures by Michael Hartnett and Seamus Heaney composed in the 1980s. Many quality haiku from Ireland were collected in the first Irish haiku magazine titled *Haiku Spirit,* edited by James Norton and Seán O'Connor, who published twenty issues between 1995 and 2000. Its demise left a void that has only been filled in recent years.

Shamrock (http://www.shamrockhaiku.webs.com), the international online magazine of the Irish Haiku Society (IHS) was founded in January 2007 and since then has published Irish and international haiku, haibun (short prose with haiku mixed in), essays and book reviews. Haiku by local authors occasionally appear in Ireland's mainstream poetry magazines such as *Poetry Ireland Review* and *Cyphers.* Quite a number of Irish haijin (haiku poets) are regular contributors to major international haiku magazines and anthologies; some of them have won accolades in various countries, including Japan, USA, Canada, Croatia, Romania, Italy and, of course, Ireland.

Four years have passed since the publication of *Bamboo Dreams.* Since then, more quality haiku have been written in Ireland, thus the need to collect this new work. In a way, *Bamboo Dreams* was a tribute to the past as well as a compilation of works created in more recent times. This new anthology reflects the recent rise of haiku popularity on our island, and brings to the attention of the reading public quite a few new names offering a look into the future. In addition to the poets showcased in *Bamboo Dreams* this collection has samples of poems by (in alphabetical order) Amanda Bell, Paul Bregazzi, Jim Burke, Paul Casey, Kara Craig, Helen Farrell Simcox, Anton Floyd, Noragh Jones, Vincent O'Connor, Eamonn T. O'Neill, Teresa O'Neill, Séamus Barra Ó Súilleabháin and Mary White.

Poets from the North of Ireland featured prominently in *Bamboo Dreams* and this is also the case with this new anthology. Alongside such authors as David Burleigh, Marion Clarke, Leo Lavery, Aine Mac Aodha, Clare McCotter, Beth McFarland and Thomas Powell, this book also introduces the Belfast poets Barbara Morton and Michael Scott. Here's one haiku by the latter:

> backlit
> by the hunter's moon
> a fallow deer

It is obvious that most Irish haiku practitioners, like their colleagues from other English-speaking countries, have chosen free-form haiku as their writing pattern. There still are a few poets, such as David Burleigh and Tony Curtis, who prefer to shape their haiku according to the 5-7-5 format, which has been abandoned by most contemporary English-language haijin. Their new works can be found in this anthology alongside the majority, which is free-form haiku.

There are currently two associations of haiku writers on this island: Haiku Ireland founded in 2004 and launched in 2005, and the Irish Haiku Society founded in September 2006. A few Irish haijin have become members of the British Haiku Society. Both societies conduct workshops and haiku-writing excursions (ginko), organise readings and book launches. The IHS website and Facebook page offer information about forthcoming haiku events and have guidelines for aspiring haijin. Since 2008 the IHS also holds the annual International Haiku Competition, which has become popular not only amongst Irish haiku aficionados but also among the international masters of the genre.

Haiku in Ireland are being written predominantly in English, although such authors as Gabriel Rosenstock, Seán Mac Mathúna and Cathal Ó Searcaigh created quite a number of quality haiku *as Gaeilge*, sometimes translating themselves into English. This anthology showcases twelve new poems by Gabriel Rosenstock, and also a selection of Irish-language haiku by Séamus Barra Ó Súilleabháin, who has regularly contributed to *Shamrock*. Here's one of his miniatures accompanied by his own translation:

> ar bhundún an chrainn ghearrtha
> déanann liréan aithris
> ar cheol sáibh shlabhraigh
>
> on a tree stump
> a lyrebird mimics
> chainsaw sounds

Despite this book being a collection of new writing, I felt the need to include a selection of haiku by the late Giovanni Malito, an Italian born in Canada who later relocated to Cork. Malito, who passed away in 2003, greatly influenced many haijin in Munster and countrywide, and his haiku, still uncollected, most definitely deserve better recognition.

As readers of this book will notice, I have mostly included haiku and not the other forms of short poetry, e.g. senryu, so nature plays a major role in the work. Robert Wilson, the former editor of *Simply Haiku*, writes:

> Once nature is removed from a haiku, it ceases to be a haiku. Without *zoka* (nature's creative spirit), words are just words, objects are just objects, everything static and unmoving like a still-borne child.[2]

In haiku writing, the use of kigo, a season word that ties a piece to a particular season, is essential, and most haiku have a kigo. A kigo-less, i.e. a season-less haiku *(muki)* is always a suspect, although we all have seen quite a few decent poems of the kind. While considering thousands of poems in search of the ones that, in my opinion, deserved to be anthologised, I realised that there's a problem haunting some of the poets: stuffing their haiku with season words, often conflicting, as they indicate different seasons. One kigo per poem is enough.

Another problem, an existential one, is excessive descriptiveness. Is the *shasei* (sketching) technique pioneered by Masaoka Shiki harming haiku? The undesirable consequence of its domination in haiku writing is that the amount of 'so what' haiku keeps growing. Yes, we comment on what we see, or have seen, but it is best to bear in mind that the end product is supposed to be a poem and not just a notebook entry preserving for posterity some little incident in our life.

Haiku, Basho's unique gift to the world, is always in danger of being replaced with meaningless or 'funny' three-liners, which are being labelled, sometimes unwittingly, sometimes shamelessly, as haiku – simply because 'haiku sell'. Too many so-called 'haiku' publications are devoid of quality writing and display next to no knowledge of the history and artistry of the genre. Haiku as an art form is a fragile flower and it needs much care.

This new anthology offers a comprehensive insight into the Irish haiku scene. At the same time it is not a compilation of poems 'about' Ireland but rather a collection of the most evocative haiku by poets born or residing here. With each passing month, more quality haiku are being written on this island, so we look forward to more haiku books and anthologies appearing in the coming years.

NOTES
1   Haruo Shirane, 'Beyond the Haiku Moment: Basho, Buson and Modern Haiku myths', *Modern Haiku*, XXXI: 1 (winter-spring 2000).
2   Robert Wilson, 'Reinventing The Wheel: The Fly Who Thought He Was a Carabao', *Simply Haiku* (Spring 2011).

BETWEEN THE LEAVES

Michael Andrew

rice picking –
grass carp
brushes ankle

dusk –
swallows weave
through bails of hay

walking to church –
the bells make the new air
colder

empty house –
the pitter-patter
of hail

daybreak –
first wind
through the oaks

stirred from a dream –
her belly
a full moon

father's old house –
his voice both here
and gone

twilight –
waves breaking
with the fisherman's casts

Amanda Bell

the midnight path
sparkles with frost –
fox crossing

beads of hail
withered almonds knocked
from the budding branch

the tang
of flowering currants –
south garden

hiding in the vine –
grape-green eyes
of the white cat

bluetit
chipping at the nut holder –
snow flurry

darting bird's foot –
the green clawed grapevine
grapples the trellis

white haze
of frost-laced windows –
cashmere layers

zigzagged by jet trails
the moon's striped face
reflects in the bay

facing down wind
over scarlet-flowered sorrel –
skylarks

spring tide –
clamshells full of sand
seagulls turn them

cloud shadows scudding
on foothills above the bay –
mottled blue lobsters

Nollaig na mBan* –
winter sun redecorates
the undressed tree

Women's Christmas in Ireland

Pat Boran

forest of seaweed
lifted by the rising tide,
gentled out of sleep

all alone at last –
the crab in the pool beside
the pool full of crabs

they lead to nothing,
the steps at the bathing hut …
then the tide comes in

maps drawn and redrawn …
the tide inching in around
the unmoved heron

this … then this … and this …
a lone crab scuttles between
islands of stillness

Paul Bregazzi

spring light
the shivering ivy
spits out a wren

nesting time –
the magpie returns
the branches to the tree

overcoat shouldered
by the kitchen chair
last night's warmth gone

October laneway
a planetarium
of fallen apples

time-jumping chipmunk
you were there
you are here

damp misty air –
even traffic sounds
this autumn morning

Jim Burke

gloomy morning
damp irises spark
in the garden

kingfisher
gathering the mid-day sun
on its wet feathers

weeding
some sort of order
in the winding path

out from the ditch
and into the ditch –
a fox's tail

Marian Burke

September tide
opening and closing the doors
of a burnt out car

PATRICK GERARD BURKE

pre-dawn
light wind
shushes through trees

autumn wind
in the lee of the oak
its shadow in leaves

September sunshine
buddleia abloom
with butterflies

through the mist ...
beechnut burrs
crackle underfoot

morning frost
writing on the windscreen
in whorls

DAVID BURLEIGH

the doorless cupboard
of a half-demolished house –
twilight in autumn

the browning edges
of the leaves of the chestnut –
un café noisette

I open a book
as the night is closing in …
the wind in autumn

after the rainfall
a squirrel takes possession
of the bowling green

over the sand dunes
where a man stares out to sea
part of a rainbow

I sit on a bench
to listen to a blackbird –
the double cherry

Paul Casey

glimpse of morning sun
ignites the spring sky
a turtledove listens

coral trees
losing hearts
all day long

drifting lotus root
breathing
the wet light

peacock spider adrift
in a gusty sea
of sunflowers

hovering peregrine
fixed above the cliff
fulcrum of shadows

Marion Clarke

reflection
in this oyster shell
pearl moon

skinny dipping –
one small step to land
on the moon

ploughed field
the warmth of his
corduroy coat

turning tide ...
a barnacle waits
on a limpet

end of day starlings blinking their return

early dawn
down at the docks
a mast nudges the moon

cold snap –
a sparrow flicks its tail
of snowflakes

Monday blues –
the thrush stops to sing
between pecks

low winter sun
warming up a row
of chimney pots

first bee
bathing its antennae
in a condensation pool

morning after –
my empty glass
full of dawn

forest mist ...
a single bee fills
the stillness

Marie Coveney

crows on a bare branch –
ink-laden
brushstrokes

a blue sky beyond
magnolia flowers
full galleon sails

Kara Craig

dandelion clock
midday shadows
grow longer

boarded up windows –
the house engulfed in
nasturtium flame

August eve by lough shore –
green algae gather
at wader's feet

steeple high above
an oak grove –
boat circles the island

bulrush feathered
with yellow pollen –
a caterpillar

descending snowflakes
the battlefield
white again

the ascent
of the orange moon –
a dinghy bobs near shore

an old spade
washed to the shore
picked up again

June sunset
ochre cliffs slide
into the ocean

All Souls Day –
night sky alive with
white flares

overgrown brambles
magpie's beak
stained purple

summer solstice
birdsong
late in the evening

Tony Curtis

a fisherman's eyes –
if you look deep into them,
they are full of poems

a wreck on the shore,
rusting back into grains of sand
wave by wave by wave

white-petaled flowers
grow on the back of the bog –
white-petaled ponies

before last night
earth was clothed in green leaf –
now all has fallen

look at the snow goose –
it imitates the snow flake,
melts away in summer

cormorant shadows,
their dark wings cleaving the air –
currachs* gone to sea

Currach (curragh): an Irish or Scottish boat made of waterproof material over a light wood frame

Patrick Deeley

raindrops on wild roses –
the stone quarry stands open
to blossom and fall

fern and celandine –
a mattress printing its own
celandine and fern

Ann Egan

water laps
stone's bed –
the river's slow dance

clover casts plum shadows ...
the bridge arches
a rainbow

buttercups
light the forgotten wayside –
sun shines on all

pale seedlings curl
beneath the oak's spread –
mother and child play

her first smile –
catkins curve across
a brook

road flowers
cast reflection on the pool –
earth reaches heaven

GILLES FABRE

first leaves –
before raking
I look at the blue sky

first to blossom
this crooked tree
in my street!

in the old iron pot
morning tea
reheated by midday sun

baby ducks
the smallest beak gets
the biggest breadcrumb

temple heron
for you
I make a cairn

mountain sunset –
among the pines
one read-leaved tree

winter dusk –
old man with a limp
walks a limping dog

through the bus window
opened to greet a friend,
first snow

seagull
on the weather-vane
shaped as a shark

on ice, next to
the farmed ones, the salmon
that have swum the ocean

ocean breeze
easing three or four seagulls
through the goal posts

beyond this blossom
entrapped in snow,
a world of sound and fury

Helen Farrell Simcox

castle ruins
framed in stone
crescent moon

dawn slumber –
cawing of a tone deaf crow
shatters silence

early morning bliss
the scent of honeysuckle
and birdsong

scent of bonfires
through leafless trees –
harvest moon

Anton Floyd

arrowhead leaves
in the flickering wind
shoals of fish

waiting
in the sheaths of ice
blades of grass

emerald fish
break surface
a stippling glaze

wren song
filling the frozen valley
the ping of crystal

the wind
spilling starlings
into the sky

cooing pigeons
from the branches
bubbles of woodwind

wild geese
veering north
on the starmap

bluebell wood
footprint
of the sky

against the window
the fly's filigree wings
the gauze of rain

on dark foliage
jasmine flowers sip
the starlight

a sudden slit
in the papery sky –
golden ink spilt

William Gibb Forsyth

storm clouds –
seaweed sways
as the seal passes

sunrise
fish in shallow water
escape the darkness

Michael Gallagher

rainy day
not even the postman tempts
the dog outdoors

reflections quiver
in the pool
willow branches

icy path –
hesitant hops
of a thrush

Patricia Groves

concrete wall
rusting shamrock
stains the flaking paint

of the billion stars
this one
the dawn-bringer

Francis Harvey

I have closed my eyes
the better the hear the swish
of a passing bird

sleeping, I think of
Errigal and Mount Fuji …
the shape of my dreams

snow, and the old man
listens to the rafters creak –
the weight of winter

long before I hear
him I see his precursor –
the cuckoo flower

the best of the day:
sweet nothing exchanged between
a blackbird and me

Noragh Jones

heavy May afternoon
each insect
doing its own buzzing

a power of stillness –
stone tree
in a cloud of midges

old grey cat and I
sharing a can of sardines
he winks I wink back

shifting shadows
stone beings hunkered
on the black bog

in the lounge bar
a grinning cheese plant
lies in wait

dandelion clock
the child's cheeks balloon
and time takes wing

beyond the ha ha
a pheasant struts
among the lambs

rainbow trout leaps
in the mirrored loch
a rippling grace note

unattended moment
sunbeams thick with
faded mysteries

a morning
so still
you can hear the silence

already the spiders
weaving new locks
on the emptied woodshed

under the spare room mattress
three dried bats
their weightless death

DAVID J. KELLY

summer evening
dusk falling
through the skylight

all across the lake
summer stirring
beneath swallows' wings

passing crows
the flap of ragged fabric
in a freshening breeze

circling
around cone-heavy pines
goldcrest song

first rain
the country lane's secrets
spoken aloud

windy day
my thoughts turn
on prayer wheels

flightless …
the moth still faces
the flame

as dusk settles,
silhouettes slip free
of their shadows

sunspots …
within the bright light
something brighter

Paddy's Day
a patch of green
on Ireland's Eye

heavy skies …
as hills weep into valleys
salmon leaping

cherry blossoms
I recall your happiness
in that photograph

Noel King

derelict convent –
black and white little bird
on the windowsill

discarded Barbie
water seeping
through her limbs

between the rain clouds,
yellow furze
atop the hill

a pointing spire –
the purples and blues
of the winter sky

house deserted –
rhubarb stumps
in the back garden

a potato mound –
old ship sails
keep it dry

a lettuce head
curling to its heart –
the only one unplucked

rainy summer over –
the hatchet handle
loose

on the roof trusses
in the old factory
owls waiting

the Battalion tailor
repairing the suits
nibbled by birds

ladybird hiking
on the road of the blade –
secateurs

dusk thickens
bats disturb
choral evensong

Anatoly Kudryavitsky

spring tide –
the reflection of a bridge
flows under the bridge

their branches almost touch …
glass-house cherry tree
and the one outside

evening lull
a seaside cave exhaling
butterflies

mosquito
in Baltic amber –
its frozen flight

boundary stone –
the nettles
pause

streaming
along the disused road,
a river of mist

ventilator off –
the sound of dragonfly
wing beats

on the steps
of the Freedom Memorial,
a discarded snake skin

moonlight
through thorny trees –
a scarlet tanager

inside the empty shell, snail's dreams

midnight lake
the silver of
yester moons

long boats
more firewood
toward sunrise

Leo Lavery

tall tombstones
trembling
with time

in the sun
the paper-white
pink roses

not suddenly
but still –
the snail!

the blackbird as usual
when I was about to
buttonhole God

on
the miser's grave
gold dandelions

sunny spring morning
even the newcome phone bill
appears beautiful

rainbow
I stand astonished-
vanished

blackbird!
so very kind of you encoring
after the thunderstorm

on the fast lane
of the re-opened motorway
snail-tracks

snow
stretching fields
far farther out

Halloween
scenting stars
this Earth evening

snow
a black cat
hogs the landscape

Mark Lonergan

autumnal dusk
a fading light
in his workshop

late Autumn
a lone elm leaf
hanging on

dark wintry sky
geese wedge their way
into the wind

watercolour class –
everyone begins
with light blue

torrential rain
umbrellas mushroom
in the park

July deluge
lawn sprinkler
joins in

AINE MAC AODHA

sudden downpour –
spring's late tadpoles
darting in a pool

Séan Mac Mathúna

in this forest
listening to
ten thousand years of rain

in midday heat
owls recall
the cool moons

stormy morning –
wet sheepdogs
outsmell the lilacs

burning an old keel –
mackerel spawning
in the chimney

rural prison –
larksong drawing up faces
from the yard

museum at night –
whelk shells still strain
for the racing tides

mad for colour
the river
rushes towards Red Canyon

wilds of Kerry –
creaking cabbages
dripping scarecrows

roaring waterfall –
up river can't hear
down river

call of the curlew
icicles longer
life shorter

snowdrops here again
little oakwood
wake up

evening on blue mountain –
orbiting sheep
compete with the stars

Clare McCotter

evening star
rising in tall grasses
the whippet's ears

stillest night
over frozen grass
horse hooves

last frozen star
inside
a bud forsythia

the lane
turning to twilight
a bat

morning star
stunned on her palm
a gold finch

yellow moon
on the piano
the cat's shadow stills

night woods
motionless
the dog listens

barren hill
howling at a full moon
thorn tree

river deep
in night's amethyst heart
otter song

first star –
stitching blue dusk
a bat

old mare
winter's depth
in her black mane

rags of hill snow
unmoved in roaring waters
a heron's throat

Joe McFadden

October evening
wind carries
the smell of rain

Beth McFarland

visible
between the photos,
what didn't happen

measuring a life
from crocus
to crocus

finally
the old man's apples
left for the birds

morning mist
magnifying
the singing

the first lemon yellow
fluttering
we change direction

accepting the day
the sun blazes colour
into my eyelids

I remember
what I thought I'd forgotten –
the plum tree blossoms

a mouse
in its forest home –
dreams of spring rain

light reflected
on an uneven wall –
all that matters

summer nights –
the traffic outside
a familiar lullaby

summer storm –
between the maize fields
a strip of heat

tremor
in the moth's wing –
remembering the dream

Séan McWilliams

in clear water
a trout
between sky and gravel

derelict station –
wooden benches with forever
carved in hearts

potter's wheel –
each individual piece
from the same clay

in the fading light
invisible hands
juggle midges

winter evening –
I turn off the TV
to watch the fire

outgoing tide –
every pebble
in its place

in the dog's dish
early this morning
a scrap of moon

cigarette break –
taking a close-up
of a scented rose

foggy morning:
putting faces to voices
on the radio

waxing moon –
the ribbon water
drapes round a rock

in spring
the cry of a cuckoo –
someone else's dream

at twilight
daffodils colour
the blackbird's song

Giovanni Malito

on the lake
listening to the loon
after it's gone

wind blowing
out to sea
part of me follows

bumblebees
yellowed with pollen
and sun

thunderstruck oak ...
the long line of ants
departing at dusk

sparrows
and a derelict
sharing the alley

the sound
of warming air ...
spring approaches

spring in the meadow
and near me, one flower buzzes
while another hums

clear night –
in the space of a smile
the meteor is gone

butterflies
stitching
grass to air

polished wood
shimmering
with apparitions

nearly black   the odour of damp earth

abandoned fairgrounds …
faint screams come whistling
through the autumn air

lone blackbird
in the far away sky –
all of it

Máire Morrissey-Cummins

sky ablaze
with a frozen sunset
deep winter

castle ruin
propping up the walls
a Buddleia bush

birch tree
leans into its shadow
day lifting

glitters of sky
through tall tree tops
summer noon

empty playground
only cherry blossoms
on the swings

high summer —
bowing into their shadows
white oxen

cat flap
a trail of blossoms
to her bowl

snow shadows
bare branches lean
into the sunset

noon heat
raspberry canes
blush naked

graveyard visit
a spider's web glitters
in a broken vase

cradled
in a cluster of stars –
new moon

winter rain
each droplet a window
to the sky

BARBARA MORTON

colder days …
walnut trees yet in leaf
in the dying light

sun low in the sky –
warm grass swarms
with grasshoppers

against sunset wall
autumn brushwood stacked
away from the wind

small shrine
a blue prayer flag among
stubbles of thistle

James Norton

August heat –
faint click of pine cones
opening as we part

the news –
across rippling wheat
shadows scythe

sea light
outracing the wind
a raptor

icy new year
at the tip of bull island
crescent moon

salt whitened
remains of a sand-hare
spirited away

rare fish-flake
all the way from Japan
for a stray cat

dinner *alfresco*
serenaded from the rooftop
by a cricket

leaf drip –
an invisible roofer tap-taps
nails into fog

sea fog:
a boxful of fisheyes
staring at nothing

walking from shadow
his face for a moment sunlit
this stranger

between tenements
red ball of sun:
she hobbles on home

Christmas Night:
in the Chinese girl's window
a longing-lamp

Sean O'Connor

halting everything
this hazel wood
those four cows

awake in dawn silence –
suddenly
many birds singing

silence
these weathered stones
speak

cloud and stone
just cloud and stone
light

out of darkness
at the edge of these woodlands,
wild magnolia

Bull Island fog
hearing the fog horn's
absence

dense winter fog
how purple
this beggar's hands

arriving
from darkness
the sound of crickets

cold morning
the bamboo grove
groaning

in this late night
a fallen silver beech
almost azure

white plum tree
its blossoms
touching stars

mountain thunder
silencing
a thousand cicadas

Terry O'Connor

autumn mist
in the beggar's hand –
his empty stare

rushing for the train ...
usually I'd take care
to avoid a snail

escape ...
the grey heron
dripping twilight

mushrooms
the door
ajar

the calm before ...
this old fishing boat
anchored to the moon

startling a feather
from an empty branch ...
winter rain

sunlight
dappling the silence
of a forest trail

blank document –
staring the clouds
into shapes

moonlight –
tracing the blue shadow
of a white tree

filling my lungs
in the pine wood
trunks of sunlight

a perfect moon ...
only pennies
in her begging bowl

wedding day
the swirling of swallows
round the sycamore tree

Vincent O'Connor

rippling air
the cocooned butterfly
hears sky

spring dawn
the cat presents
a silent robin

heat haze
a butterfly attempts
to land again

birthday barbeque –
a murmuring of starlings
cloud the horizon

on the lapping shore
four moons
rising

the evening
slowly gathering
trees

a flash of moon
her long hair
almost grey

cloudburst –
sudden scattering
of starlings

on the way home
the moon
stopping at every light

darting
between leaves
blue rain

another full moon
our doctors advise
stop trying

through the window
paper lanterns –
lifting my dad into bed

Hugh O'Donnell

sunset on Gloucester Lane –
concrete bollards
in railing shadow twine

shadowland –
around the ash
a circle of black leaves

a free-for-all
in the willow arch –
sparrow convention

gull dispute –
sun rises
in an office window

dawn –
moon rests on the outstretched
arm of the crane

pre-dawn
security light –
fox patrol

first of May –
a fingertip of moon
on the skylight

heatwave –
in the pond tadpoles
simmering

after rain
half a dozen pigeons
making ripples

hauliers –
birdsong winching up
the sun!

worksite in moonlight
fox cubs playing chase
on a hill of sand

auction –
a smell of horse
where the horse has been

Siofra O'Donovan

washing clothes
in the cold mountain stream –
buttons flash

an owl glides
over the black tree –
moon stands stock still

pilgrims on their way home –
rain falling
on the mud path

a thousand flags flapping
in the cool morning air –
monkeys climb the hill

under the Dhauladar rocks,
a stony path
to the market

down the Ganges
on an old wooden boat –
sun sinks under water

Nora O'Dwyer

red fox
his gaze
through the glass

whistling wind –
a new starling nest
in my house vent

windy boreen* –
cock pheasant puffed out
in search of his destiny

* Boreen: unpaved rural road in Ireland.

Mary O'Keeffe

autumn odyssey
a ladybird enters the
swallows' nest

spring frost
a puff of cirrus
swept from the moon's mouth

choppy waves
a young concertina player
juggling a hornpipe

last autumn's leaves
cartwheeling
through the still May dawn

winter solstice
the footsteps of a missing dog
return

Eamonn T. O'Neill

low winter sun
the blindness
of my shadow

out of the morning mist
a mountain arrives
after the mail man

empty harbour
i walk through the uneasiness
of gulls

winter moon a pale tide through my window

evening mist
a swan drifts towards
eternity

coastal storm
a wave breaks
over the moon

Teresa O'Neill

at the water's edge
marsh marigolds
spilling yellow

christening day
flavour of wild garlic
on Teapot Lane

tide out
a shell duck family
hoover up the snails

KATE O'SHEA

harvest moon
flour sprinkled
to catch a mouse

tiny raspberries
a cool river widens
spring thaw

seagulls wheedle
through columns of salt water –
fishing trawler

eye of potato –
a corner of the garden
blinks in dusty sun

splash of raindrops –
a cat under rhubarb leaves
looks out

Séamus Barra Ó Súilleabháin

ar dhromchla na mara
eitlíonn ealaí
os cionn scamall

(on the sea surface,
swans flying
above the clouds)

seasann faoileán
ar bharr an tséipéil fholaimh
ag breathnú ar an lá

(a gull
atop the empty church
watching the day go by)

idir an moncaí
agus an duine
a scáil uisce

(between the monkey
and the spectator
their reflections)

seanfhear
is a pháirc
níos glaise ag cuimhní

(old man's field
greener
in his memory)

thíos anseo
canaid don doircheacht
na míolta móra

(down below
singing to the darkness
great whales)

scáil na ré
ar chrithloinnir –
fuaim toinne

(moon's reflection
quivering –
sound of waves)

léas na gealaí
éiríonn seiceamar aosta
níos dorcha arís

(moonlight
the old sycamore
looks darker)

sa gharraí úr
liú aonair capaill
leoithne earraigh

(in the field
a solitary horse cry –
spring breeze)

an solas múchta
calóga sneachta ag sileadh
sa chiúnas

(lights out –
snowflakes fall
into silence)

fionnuaire –
fanann seatlaí óg
le taoscán féir

(cool breeze –
the shetland pony waits
for a load of hay)

ar bhundún an chrainn ghearrtha
déanann liréan aithris
ar cheol sáibh shlabhraigh

(on a tree stump
a lyrebird mimics
chainsaw sounds)

an Teampaillín Bán
an tost á ghardáil
ag crann iúir

(a famine graveyard
silence guarded
by a yew tree)

Maeve O'Sullivan

May breeze
blowing this field of dandelions
to one o'clock

Saturday morning:
spring sunshine
on the moving mill wheel

choppy Irish Sea
failing to dislodge
this red starfish

balmy afternoon
on the estuary –
a boat horn sounds

ripening equally
on both sides of the Blackwater –
blackberries

tall ash tree   the smell of last night's fire

limestone outcrop:
a wall of wild garlic
emits its signature

these stone walls
hemming him in too –
cinnabar caterpillar

cloudy afternoon …
my sweet pea flowers
becoming peas

autumn deluge
making a giant slug trail
of these midland fields

Palacio Real:
a blackbird forages
in the shade of a maze

All Souls' Day:
moving shadows
of wind-blown prayer flags

Thomas Powell

cool of the moon
a snail's shape
crosses the patio

sun-touched gully ...
the wool and bones
of a passing winter

sunlit oak stump
a zebra spider
jumps through time

freezing fog
a dog barks from where
the fox was heading

New Year's Day
the glare of two suns
along a flood plain

crumbling chimney ...
sunlight warms
the turf cutter's hearth

golden light
returning the silhouettes
of brent geese

above the contour
of ebbing snow
two red kites

tumbling canopy ...
the delicate calls
of coal tits

ripples along
the lough shore
a dunnock's song

following
the drumlin's curve
a pine's shadow

dormant heather
a wren ticks into
another year

Isabelle Prondzynski

empty fountain
refilling with slush –
first birdsong

ripples of gold –
jacaranda leaflets
against the sky

church window –
Christ reaching out
through metal bars

midsummer night –
sun rises
where it sets

hazy morning –
thorn tree flowers sprinkled
round the bus stop

one by one
the roofs lose their colour –
summer sunset

evening cool –
the fish fryer's fire
glows from afar

out into daylight –
surprised mango larva
raising its head

late dawn –
even a grey sunrise
raises the sun

alone and bowed –
the brown autumn thistle
amidst golden leaves

winter butterfly –
the tickling sensation
in my hand

Christmas moon
dogs out sniffing
in the snow

Mark Roper

Victoria Lock –
first through the opened gates
a swallow

evening road –
long after a car's gone by,
scent of tobacco

Gabriel Rosenstock

scol an loin
ag éag –
cór an tsráidbhaile

(the blackbird's call
fades away –
village choir)

miotas is ea an t-am –
sliabh
sa loch

(time is a myth –
a mountain
in a lake)

gan gíocs ná míocs –
lúbann an bamboo
don cheolaire caschoille

(without creaking –
the bamboo bends
for a bush warbler)

fothrach mainistreach …
monabhar na gaoithe
nach gcloiseann éinne

(ruined abbey …
the murmuring wind
that nobody hears)

móin inné
feamainn inniu –
saol asail

(yesterday turf
seaweed today –
the life of a donkey)

greim orthu
níl ag na flaithis –
géanna sneachta

(heaven
has no hold on them –
snow geese)

iompraíonn sé ina choir
rúin na deargmhaidine –
coileach

(in his comb he carries
secrets of the red dawn –
rooster)

marbhán i ngort
na scamaill, ámh,
ní mhoillíonn

(dead man in a field
but the clouds
pause not)

foirmiú oighir –
eaglais dhia gan
trócaire

(ice formation –
the church of god
the merciless)

géimneach ar dtús
ansin na hadharca –
ba ag teacht amach as an gceo

(a soft lowing
and then the horns –
cows coming out of the mist)

oighearchaidhp –
imíonn fiolar mara as radharc
san uaigneas

(ice cap
a white-tailed eagle vanishes
in loneliness)

mám agus scrín:
scamaill anoir
scamaill aniar

(mountain pass and shrine:
clouds from the east
clouds from the west)

Adam Rudden

queue outside the book shop –
footprints line up
snow's typography

Michael Scott

June rain –
waste ground awash
with poppies

morning meadow –
above the mist
the backs of cattle

tide on the turn
estuary driftwood
chops and churns

the oaks he planted
tall enough
to steal his shadow

dense forest floor
along the rotting trunk
a row of saplings

river divides
the island granted
right of way

sea trout running –
leaves swirling past the lure
outpace the stream

last rook leaves
gleaned corn field
empty

closing the skylight
he almost traps
the evening star

backlit
by the hunter's moon
a fallow deer

weak winter sun
mist from the river
delays its rise

new year dawns
last night's prints
overprinted with frost

John W. Sexton

one breath
on the dandelion clock …
I set my garden

bitter morning
the first sloe
furs my tongue

a still morning
the cuckoo naming itself
out of sight

daddy-long-legs
from this cage of fingers
up into moonlight

slow morning
the mountains lessening
in the rain

late afternoon
a fading photograph of sky
on the tin roof

singing until only
the distance can hear him
skylark

morning breeze
garden oak throwing shadows
into itself

sudden breeze
so light the fir trees
heavy with rain

moonlight
the snowman
whiter

pines on the far hill
holding the distance
in place

sunrise –
a pebble sinking through
the snowman's face

Eileen Sheehan

muddied earth spring happening elsewhere

summer storm
wind chimes silenced
by the noise of wind

just when I thought
my luck was turning
lone magpie

long road
the leaves and I
windblown

plucking a white hair
from my eyebrow
crescent moon

October morning
spiderweb
snares sunlight

absent moon
clouds amber
in streetlight

winter morning
in the dark drawer
spring bulbs unplanted

cathedral spire
a star held in the arms
of the cross

frosty night
our breaths touching
the moon

Breid Sibley

woodland
chorus ascends
to greet sunrise

scent of sweet pea
embroidery
of flowers

Bee Smith

soft rain
falling on our
unhurried steps

in from a blizzard
our cat
head-bumps affection

moth perches on my pillow –
sleepier than me
this restless night

Martin Vaughan

slant light
a newborn calf shivers
into life

geese ahoy!
a score of tiny shadows
flit across the strand

first flush of warmth
butterflies
fooled out of slumber

sun slung low
thistledown strays in
from neighbouring lawns

dusk!
the scent of horse piss
marking the right of way

distant thunder –
the river quickens
with expectation

heatwave!
this long road
must lead somewhere

white moon on water
two swans
by the riverbank

mountain fog –
bleached sheep skull
on snow

autumn
a purple thistle crown
rising over barley

last leaf on rowan tree
the wind won't
leave it alone

New Years Day
I watch loved ones recede to
silver speck of sky

Aisling White

deserted beach
sands race out
to shore

spring dew
on a spider's web –
communion veil

soft rain
in every droplet
a million days

summer meadow –
the sea breeze
hushed by lark song

forest gloom
sigh of the wind
in the towering pines

monastic high cross –
on one arm, a robin,
on the other, the moon

beach sunrise
the fog returns
a dog's bark

shop window –
sparkling in the dark,
Orion's reflection

Mary White

sinking sun –
a hum of heat
from the rocks

swimming
towards the full moon …
my silent song

thirty years gone
my mother's magnolia blooms
filling the sky

steely calm
a heron and a cormorant
each on his own rock

About the Authors

MICHAEL ANDREW (Andrew Michael O'Brien) is from Westport, County Mayo. He published his haiku in *Shamrock* and in the *Bamboo Dreams* anthology, and was a runner-up in the Mainichi Daily News Haiku Contest 2009 (Japan). He is a member of the IHS.

AMANDA BELL is a freelance editor living in Dublin. Her poetry, haiku and haibun have appeared in *Shamrock, cattails, Presence, Blithe Spirit, The Stinging Fly, Crannóg, The Burning Bush 2, The Ofi Press Literary Magazine* and *The Clearing*. She is a member of the IHS. A collection of her haiku and related forms, *Undercurrent*, was published in 2016.

PAT BORAN was born in Portlaoise and lives in Dublin. He has published a dozen collections of poetry, prose and translations. His latest volume of poems, *The Next Life*, came out in 2012 and his collection of haiku, *Waveforms*, was published in 2015. His haiku have also appeared in *Shamrock* and the *Bamboo Dreams* anthology.

PAUL BREGAZZI is a primary school teacher from west Dublin. His poems have appeared in *Crannóg, Revival, The Stinging Fly, The Stony Thursday Book;* his haiku in *Shamrock*. In 2015, one of his haiku was shortlisted for the Touchstone Award for Individual Poems. He is a member of the IHS.

JIM BURKE is a native of Limerick. His poems have appeared in *The Literary Bohemian, Crannog, The Revival* and *The Stony Thursday Book*, of which he was a co-founder (with John Liddy). His haiku have been published in *Shamrock*. He is a member of the IHS.

MARIAN BURKE is from County Galway, now living in Dublin. She is a member of Haiku Ireland.

PATRICK GERARD BURKE is from Cork. He is an Anglican priest and currently rector of Castlecomer Union of parishes in County Kilkenny. In the late 1990s, he was active on the Shiki

Internet Haiku Salon website where he published some of his haiku. His haiku have also appeared in *Shamrock* and the *Bamboo Dreams* anthology.

DAVID BURLEIGH was born in Northern Ireland and lives in Japan. He co-translated *A Hidden Pond: Anthology of Modern Haiku* (1997, revised 2003). His most recent chapbook collection is *RC* (2009). His haiku have appeared in the *Bamboo Dreams* anthology.

PAUL CASEY was born in Cork in 1968 and lived for many years in Southern Africa. His début collection is *home more or less* (Salmon Poetry, 2012), followed by Virtual Tides (Salmon, 2016). He is poet in residence each year during the Bealtaine festival in elderly homes around County Cork, and the founder/director of the Ó Bhéal reading series in Cork city. His haiku have appeared in *Shamrock*.

MARION CLARKE is from County Down. She writes poetry and short stories. Her haiku have been published in *Shamrock, The Heron's Nest, Notes from the Gean* and *A Hundred Gourds,* as well as in the *Bamboo Dreams* anthology. She is a member of the IHS, and won 2nd prize in the IHS International Haiku Competition 2015.

MARIE COVENEY is from County Cork. She has had poems published in *Poetry Review, The SHOp, Southword,* and her haiku appeared in *Shamrock*. She is a member of the IHS.

KARA CRAIG is originally from Bellaghy, County Derry, now living in Dublin. She is a member of the IHS and has published her haiku in *Shamrock*.

TONY CURTIS was born in Dublin and now lives in Balbriggan, County Dublin. He has published seven collections of mainstream poetry, as well as *Crossings: 21 Bridges* (2004), *Sand Works* (2011) and *Arran Currach* (2013), which are collections of his haiku. His haiku also appeared in the *Bamboo Dreams* anthology.

PATRICK DEELEY is a native of Loughrea, County Galway. He works as a teacher in Ballyfermot in Dublin. He has authored eight collections of poems, the latest title being *Groundswell: New and Selected Poems* (2013), as well as books for young people. His haiku were published in the *Bamboo Dreams* anthology.

ANN EGAN was born in County Laois and lives in County Kildare. Her poetry books are *Landing the Sea* (Bradshaw Books, 2003); *The Wren Woman* (The Black Mountain Press, 2003) and *Telling Time* (Bradshaw Books, 2012). Her haiku have been published in *Shamrock* and the *Bamboo Dreams* anthology.

GILLES FABRE was born in France and lives in Ireland. He started writing haiku in the 1990s and published them in *Haiku Spirit, Presence* and *Blithe Spirit,* as well as in *The New Haiku* anthology (Snapshot Press) and the *Bamboo Dreams* anthology. His collection *Because of the Seagull* (The Fishing Cat Press) appeared in 2005. He is the editor of the Haiku Spirit site, www.haikuspirit.org (not to be confused with the haiku magazine of the same name).

HELEN FARRELL SIMCOX lives in County Cork. A member of the IHS and Haiku Ireland, she has had her haiku published in *Shamrock*.

ANTON FLOYD was born in Egypt and raised in the Middle-East. He studied at Trinity College, Dublin and UCC, and later lived and worked in the eastern Mediterranean. He is now living in West Cork and teaching in Cork City. His poems appeared in *The Stony Thursday Book* and his haiku in *Shamrock*. He won the IHS International Competition (2014) and was runner up in the Snapshot Press Haiku Calendar 2016 Competition. He is a member of the IHS.

WILLIAM GIBB FORSYTH is originally from East Lothian in Scotland, now living in Bray, County Wicklow. A member of the IHS, he has published his haiku in *Shamrock*.

MICHAEL GALLAGHER was born on Achill Island, County Mayo and now lives in County Kerry. He writes poems and short stories and has been published in *The Doghouse Book of Ballad Poems*. His haiku appeared in *Frogpond, Crannóg, World Haiku Review, Shamrock* and the *Bamboo Dreams* anthology. He is a member of the IHS.

PATRICIA GROVES is a script writer and biographer. Her biography of Anna Parnell, *Petticoat Rebellion: The Anna Parnell Story*, was published by Mercier Press. She is a member of the IHS and her haiku have appeared in *Shamrock*.

FRANCIS HARVEY was born in Enniskillen, County Fermanagh, in 1925 and lived in Donegal until his death in 2014. He authored a number of poetry collections. His book titled *Donegal Haiku* was published by Dedalus in 2013.

NORAGH JONES was born in Belfast and has long been living in Wales with her husband, the late and sadly missed haiku poet Ken Jones. Her haiku and haibun have appeared in such publications as *Blithe Spirit* and *Presence*. Her collection of haiku and haibun titled *Stone Circles* was published in 2004. She is a member of the British Haiku Society and the Red Thread Haiku group.

DAVID J. KELLY is a Dubliner and a researcher. Having started writing haiku in 2007, he has had his haiku, senryu, tanka, haibun and haiga published in *Blithe Spirit, Presence, Notes from the Gean, Haiku Journal, Shamrock, A Hundred Gourds*, etc. He is a member of the British Haiku Society and Haiku Ireland.

NOEL KING is a native of Tralee, County Kerry. He has worked as an arts administrator, a journalist, fundraiser and performer with The Bunratty Singers. His haiku have appeared in *Presence, Shamrock* and the *Bamboo Dreams* anthology. His first poetry collection, *Prophesying the Past*, was published in 2010, his second, *A Stern Wave*, in 2013, and his third, *Sons*, in 2015, all from Salmon Poetry.

ANATOLY KUDRYAVITSKY is a founding member and the current chairman of the IHS and editor of *Shamrock*. His haiku have appeared in *Presence, World Haiku Review, Roadrunner, A Hundred Gourds,* etc. His collections of haiku, *Morning at Mount Ring* (2007) and *Capering Moons* (2011; shortlisted for the Touchstone Distinguished Haiku Book Award 2011), were published by Doghouse Books. His new collection of haiku, *Horizon*, is forthcoming from Red Moon Press (USA). He won the Suruga Baika Prize (2008) and the Vladimir Devidé Award (2012 and 2014), and edited an earlier anthology of haiku from Ireland titled *Bamboo Dreams* (Doghouse, 2012; shortlisted for the Touchstone Distinguished Haiku Book Award 2012). He lives in Dublin.

LEO LAVERY was born in Lisburn, County Antrim. Educated at Queen's University, Belfast, he worked as a teacher, mostly abroad. He has published two collections of his poems. His haiku have appeared in *Blithe Spirit* and other magazines, as well as in the *Bamboo Dreams* anthology.

MARK LONERGAN is originally from Limerick but now resides on the north side of Dublin. He published his haiku in *The Heron's Nest, Paper Wasp* and *Shamrock*, as well as in the *Bamboo Dreams* anthology. *Shamrock* also published his essays on haiku. He is a member of Haiku Ireland. In 2010 he won the Touchstone Award for an individual haiku.

AINE MAC AODHA is from Omagh, County Tyrone. Her latest collection of poems titled *Landscape of Self* was published by Lapwing Press, Belfast, in 2013. Her haiku have appeared in *Shamrock* and the *Bamboo Dreams* anthology. She is a member of the IHS.

SÉAN MAC MATHÚNA was born in Tralee, County Kerry, and now lives in Dublin. He writes in both English and Irish. He has published two collections of short stories, as well as plays, the latest being *Duilleoga Tae* (Arlen House, 2015). His haiku have appeared in *Lishanu* and in the *Bamboo Dreams* anthology.

CLARE MCCOTTER lives in County Derry and works as a psychiatric nurse. Her haiku, tanka and haibun have appeared in *Frogpond, Presence, Blithe Spirit, Roadrunner, World Haiku Review, Modern Haiku, Simply Haiku* and *Shamrock*. She also contributed to the *Bamboo Dreams* anthology. A member of the British Haiku Society, she authored a collection of haiku and related poems titled *Black Horse Running* (2012). She won first prize in the IHS haiku competition 2010 and 2011.

JOE MCFADDEN is a Dubliner and a member of Haiku Ireland. He has contributed to *Haiku Spirit* and *Red Thread Haiku*, writing articles, book reviews and compiling a haiku bibliography. His haiku have appeared on the Haiku Spirit website and in the *Bamboo Dreams* anthology.

BETH MCFARLAND is from County Tyrone, currently based in Germany. Her haiku have appeared in *Heron's Nest, Blithe Spirit, A Hundred Gourds, Chrysanthemum* and *Shamrock*, as well as in the *Bamboo Dreams* anthology. She is a member of the IHS and the British Haiku Society. She won honourable mention in the IHS International Haiku Competition 2011.

SÉAN MCWILLIAMS is from Belfast. He is a member of the British Haiku Society. His haiku have appeared in *Presence, Blithe Spirit* and *Poetry Ireland Review*.

GIOVANNI MALITO (1957–2003) was Canadian of Italian descent who later relocated to Cork. He wrote poetry, haiku, prose and essays, and edited *The Brobdingnagian Times*, a publication of international poetry. His haiku appeared in

Frogpond, Blithe Spirit, The Heron's Nest and the *Bamboo Dreams* anthology.

MAIRE MORRISEY-CUMMINS was born in Tramore, County Waterford and now resides in County Wicklow. She is a member of both the IHS and Haiku Ireland. Her haiku have appeared in *Shamrock* and the *Bamboo Dreams* anthology. She won honourable mention in the IHS Haiku Competition 2010.

BARBARA MORTON is from Belfast. Her poems have been published in *The SHOp, The Stinging Fly, Burning Bush II, The Yellow Nib, Abridge* and *An Sionnach,* her haiku in *Shamrock.* She is a member of the British Haiku Society.

JAMES NORTON was born in Dublin where he still lives. In 1995 he founded *Haiku Spirit,* a printed Irish journal of haiku and related forms and was the sole editor of it until 1997. His own haiku have appeared in *Hundred Haiku* (Iron Press, 1991), in various journals such as *Blithe Spirit, Presence, Shamrock* and *Poetry Ireland Review,* and in the *Bamboo Dreams* anthology. His haiku collections are *Words on the Wind* published in 1997 and *The Fragrance of Dust* published in 2012. He is a member of both Haiku Ireland and the Red Thread Haiku group.

SEÁN O'CONNOR is a Dubliner. Between 1998 and 2000 he co-edited *Haiku Spirit* with James Norton. His haiku have appeared there, in *Blithe Spirit* and in *Shamrock,* as well as in *The New Haiku, Zen Poems* and the *Bamboo Dreams* anthologies. He has published a joint collection of haiku, *Pilgrim Foxes* (2001), with Jim Norton and Ken Jones. In 2016 he published a collection of haiku and haibun, *Let Silence Speak.*

TERRY O'CONNOR is from Galway. He won the Vancouver Cherry Blossom Festival Invitational Haiku Contest in 2009. His haiku have appeared in *The Heron's Nest, Simply Haiku, Notes from the Gean* and *Shamrock,* as well as in the *Bamboo Dreams* anthology. He is a member of the IHS.

VINCENT O'CONNOR is originally from Kilfinane, County Limerick. Having lived and worked in Spain and Japan, he now lives in Cork where he manages a language centre and is currently completing a masters degree. He is a member of the IHS. His haiku have appeared in *Frogpond, Modern Haiku, A Hundred Gourds, Shamrock, Asahi Shimbun, Mainichi Shimbun,* and his other poems in *Acorn* and *Bones*.

HUGH O'DONNELL, a native of Dublin, published his haiku in *Shamrock* and in the *Bamboo Dreams* anthology. A member of the IHS, he was the winner of the *Shamrock* Readers' Choice Award 2009 and a runner-up in 2014. He also won honourable mention in the IHS haiku competition 2010. He has published three collections, the most recent being *No Place Like It* (Doghouse, 2010).

SIOFRA O'DONOVAN was born and lives in County Wicklow, where she teaches creative writing. She is a novelist, a haiku poet and a founding member of the IHS. In 2006, she worked as writer-in-residence for County Louth. She won honourable mention in the Samhain International Haiku Competition 2005. Her haiku appeared in the *Bamboo Dreams* anthology.

NORA O'DWYER is from County Tipperary and currently lives in County Kerry where she works as a tour-guide and as a translator. Her haiku have been published in *Shamrock*.

MARY O'KEEFFE is a musician and a music teacher from County Cork. A member of the IHS, she published her haiku in *Shamrock* and in the *Bamboo Dreams* anthology. She was the winner of the IHS International Haiku Competition 2009, and won the *Shamrock* Readers Choice Award for her haiku published in 2015.

EAMONN T. O'NEILL is from Dublin. His haiku have appeared in *Shamrock,* his tanka in several *Bright Star* tanka anthologies. He is a member of the IHS.

TERESA O'NEILL is from County Leitrim where she works in the educational field. Her haiku have been published in *Shamrock*.

KATE (KAREN) O'SHEA is from Dublin. Her poems have been published in *Acorn*, her haiku in *Shamrock* and the *Bamboo Dreams* anthology. She is a member of the IHS.

SÉAMUS BARRA Ó SÚILLEABHÁIN was born in London and grew up in North Kerry. He was the winner of the 2011 All Ireland Poetry Slam. His haiku have appeared in *Shamrock*. He has also published his haiku under the name Buachalán Buí (meaning yellow ragwort in Irish).

MAEVE O'SULLIVAN is from Dublin. Her haiku and senryu have appeared in various journals including *Haiku Spirit*, *Blithe Spirit*, *World Haiku Review* and *Shamrock*, as well as in the *Bamboo Dreams* anthology. Her joint collection of haiku with Kim Richardson, *Double Rainbow*, was published in 2005, followed by her solo collections, *Initial Response* (2011) and *A Train Hurtles West* (2015). She is a member of Haiku Ireland and the British Haiku Society.

THOMAS POWELL hails from Wales and is currently living in County Armagh. His haiku have appeared in *Blithe Spirit*, *Presence*, *Modern Haiku*, *The Heron's Nest*, *Shamrock* as well as in the *Bamboo Dreams* anthology. He is a member of the IHS and the British Haiku Society. His collection of haiku, *Clay Moon*, is forthcoming from Snapshot Press.

ISABELLE PRONDZYNSKI is from County Westmeath and now divides her time between Belgium and Africa. Her haiku have been published in the World Kigo Database and in *Tinywords*, as well as in the *Bamboo Dreams* anthology. She is a member of the IHS.

MARK ROPER was born in Derbyshire and lives near Piltown, County Kilkenny. He has published four poetry collections, the latest being *Whereabouts* (2005). His haiku have appeared in *Shamrock* and in the *Bamboo Dreams* anthology. He is a member of the IHS.

GABRIEL ROSENSTOCK was born in Kilfinane, County Limerick and lives in Dublin. A poet and essayist, he has authored/translated over 100 books, mostly in/into the Irish language. His collection of haiku titled *Cold Moon: Erotic Haiku* appeared in 1993. Two collections of his newer haiku followed more recently, *Where Light Begins* (2012) and *Antlered Stag of Dawn* (2015). His haiku have also appeared in the *Bamboo Dreams* anthology. His two books of essays on haiku, *Haiku Enlightenment* and *Haiku: the Gentle Art of Disappearing*, were published in 2009.

ADAM RUDDEN is based in Dublin. His poems have appeared in *Poetry Ireland Review, Cyphers, Electric Acorn*, etc.; his haiku in *Shamrock*. He edited *The New Binary Press Anthology of Poetry, Volume I*, and has published four collections of poetry with Lapwing Publications, the latest being *Solar Winds and Ions* (2011).

MICHAEL SCOTT is from Belfast. He is a member of the British Haiku Society and his haiku have appeared in *Blithe Spirit*. His haiku chapbook titled *A Year about the Farm* was published in 2013.

JOHN W. SEXTON was born in England and now lives in County Kerry. His collection of haiku titled *Shadows Bloom/ Scáthanna Faoi Bhláth* with translations into Irish by Gabriel Rosenstock was published by Doghouse in 2004. His haiku have also appeared in *Modern Haiku, Frogpond, Notes from the Gean, Roadrunner, The Heron's Nest, Shamrock* and the *Bamboo Dreams* anthology. He has also published five collections of his mainstream poems and fiction.

EILEEN SHEEHAN lives in Killarney, County Kerry. She has published two collections with Doghouse Books, the latest being *Down the Sunlit Hall* (2008). Her third collection, *The Narrow Place of Souls*, is forthcoming. Her haiku appeared in *Acorn, The Heron's Nest, Haiku Scotland, Simply Haiku, Frogpond* and *Shamrock,* as well as in the *Bamboo Dreams* anthology.

BREID SIBLEY lives in County Galway. Her haiku have been published in *Shamrock* and in the *Bamboo Dreams* anthology. She is a member of the IHS and the Baffle poetry group.

BEE SMITH was born in the USA and now lives in County Cavan. Her haiku have been published in *World Haiku Review* and in *Shamrock,* as well as in the *Bamboo Dreams* anthology. She is a member of the IHS.

MARTIN VAUGHAN was born in Tipperary and lives in Dublin. A co-founder and a member of the Board of the IHS, he has published his haiku in *Shamrock*, in the *Bamboo Dreams* anthology and on the World Kigo Database (Japan). He was a runner-up in the *Shamrock* Readers' Choice Award 2008.

AISLING WHITE is from north County Dublin. An IHS member, she has published her haiku in *Shamrock*, on the World Kigo Database (Japan) and in the *Bamboo Dreams* anthology. She was a runner-up in the *Shamrock* Readers' Choice Award 2009.

MARY WHITE is from south County Dublin. She is a member of Haiku Ireland and the British Haiku Society. Her haiku and renku have appeared in *A Hundred Gourds, Mainichi Daily News, Blithe Spirit* and *Shamrock.*